MW01166486

# My Life,

# My Devotions,

# His Promises

*Tara Altheide*

MANIFOLD GRACE
Publishing House LLC

My Life, My Devotions, His Promises Vol. II
Copyright © 2017 Tara Altheide

Cover design: CreativeLogoArt
Cover photo: Kelly Dobson

ISBN:  978-1-937400-80-4

Printed in the United States of America

Published by Manifold Grace Publishing House, LLC
Southfield, Michigan 48033
www.manifoldgracepublishinghouse.com

# Dedication

Having a family that is filled with Angels who love, support and encourage me day in and day out is an absolute blessing. So imagine how overwhelmingly blessed my heart is having not one, but two families who complete my world.

I am surrounded by a group of strong, fearless and inspiring women who motivate me to be the very best I can be every single day. Being a trainer has given me the second family I never knew I always needed.

The women I am blessed to not only work with, but who I can count on for constant support, love, guidance and pushing me beyond the limits I have set for myself have truly changed my life forever.

To every woman who has set foot within the

gym, given me the chance to be a part of your life and for giving me the courage to be who I am today, this book is dedicated to you.

# Acknowledgements

Closing your heart off and keeping your soul to yourself will never allow you to grow, learn anything new, or make a difference in this world.

It is when your heart is an open door and your soul is a book for all to read, that you meet the people who will change your life forever and give you the opportunity to see how God's hands brought them right to you.

These Angels crossed my path at the exact moment they were meant to and my heart and soul were open for the taking.

Julie Wooton, the impact you have on this world and my life is greater than you will ever know. Your words always come at the right time, your texts always bring laughter to my life and your love always fills my heart with happiness. Your thoughtfulness, encouragement and support are more than I could have ever asked for. I love and appreciate you more than you could possibly imagine.

Katherine Sheahan, with the love you are always willing to share and the encouraging words you continue to bless me with, you have inspired so much of my writing. In the short time I have known you, you have taught me to always keep an open mind, pushed me to think beyond what my mind thought it was capable of and to always step out of my comfort zone, no matter how uncomfortable it may be. You have brightened my world with your vibrant soul, and I thank God every day for placing you along my journey.

Bridgette Lansu, God's hands are always so busy at work. I am so grateful He took the time to use them to bring us together. Your willingness to help, your eagerness to support me and your love that surrounds me made this journey so peaceful and enjoyable. I am excited to see all the good things that God has in store for you and the blessings He has waiting to shower down upon you. I am so honored to be able to stand right by your side, as you stand by mine, and see His plans unfold for your life.

Maya, I never would have guessed that someone who never spoke more than a few words when I met them would change my life in so many ways. But that is exactly what you did. Seeing your amazing transformation, right before my eyes, has inspired me to always be willing to change. Your generous heart has reminded me that it is always better to give than it is to receive. And your belief in me, your refusal to give up on me when I gave you every reason to and your willingness to tell me the things I never wanted to hear, but needed to, gave me the courage and strength to keep going when quitting felt like it may have been my only option. I could go on forever about how much you have changed my life, and you already know what would be written. Just know my world would be completely incomplete without you.

Patty, Debbie A and Kiwanda, your wisdom, words of advice and the gentle, but firm pushes you were so willing to give, changed my life forever. Thank you for allowing me to be a part of your journeys. Mine would never have taken this amazing turn without you. I owe so much of my success with these books to you ladies. I will forever be grateful and ask for God's blessings to surround you with every day that comes.

# Contents

Dedication ............................................. v

Acknowledgment ............................... vii

Introduction ...................................... xv

Where We are Needed Most .............. 1

Always a Reason ................................. 3

Through Him We Can ........................ 4

Through Our Eyes .............................. 6

A Chance Worth Taking ..................... 7

Perfect Timing ................................... 8

Free to Love ....................................... 10

Where Hope is Found ........................ 11

Change is Good .................................. 12

When God is Your Guide .................... 14

God is a Giver ..................................... 16

Which Way Do I Go? .......................... 17

What's Next?? .................................... 19

A Beautiful Mind ............................... 21

Never Be Lonely ................................ 23

Less Work, More Change ................... 25

The Spirit Speaks .............................. 26

His Plan Prevails ............................... 28

Never Will We Falter ......................... 29

A Heart That Loves ............................ 30

Steps of Faith .................................... 32

Only Good Thoughts ......................... 34

Move Mountains ................................... 36

A Whisper Away ................................... 37

Faith or Fear ....................................... 39

A Father's Love ................................... 41

A Moment Makes a Lifetime ............... 42

Big or Small ......................................... 43

From the Inside Out ............................ 45

Inspire with Love ................................ 47

Words of Advice .................................. 49

With All of Your Heart ......................... 51

Always Worth It .................................. 53

A Choice We Make ............................... 54

Love Takes Action ............................... 56

Refuse to Give ..................................... 57

The Light of Love ................................ 59

Where We Need to Be .......................... 61

Mean What You Say ............................ 63

Always on His Mind ............................ 64

Temptations with Purpose ................. 66

Who are You Chasing? ........................ 68

With Weakness Comes Strength ....... 70

Never Lose Hope ................................. 71

Heals Every Hurt ................................ 73

The Control is Ours ............................ 75

Already Done ...................................... 76

A Text to God ...................................... 77

More than Expected ........................... 79

Challenges Bring Change ................... 80

Expect Answers ................................. 82
Say and Receive ................................. 83
Avoid Damage ................................... 85
He Holds the Pieces ........................... 87
Our Part is Faith ................................. 88
Love is Patient ................................... 89
Blessings Come By Faith .................... 91
To Give is to Receive .......................... 92
Gifts to Share ..................................... 93
Last Words ......................................... 95
About the Author ............................... 97

# Introduction

We may think we have this thing called life all figured out. Our days are running smoothly, our hearts are happy and things just seem to be falling right into their perfect places.

But the moment it seems like we have everything together, is the very moment we begin to see the pieces that were once so secure, fall apart.

We wonder why life is so unfair and why we cannot be happy for more than a day before we are challenged in some way. Our life doesn't fall apart because it wants to hurt us. Life falls apart because we think we can handle it all on our own. We become confident in our own abilities and strength and slowly remove God from every part of it. *I know God is next to me always—*

The further away we move from God, the less

time we spend with Him and the more we depend on ourselves. And that is what will turn our world upside down. The closer we are to Him, the more we fill ourselves with His words and promises; we will see that even when challenges come our way, our world will always feel right side up.

My Life, My Devotions, HIS PROMISES helped you begin your walk with God. In volume 2, you will find even more ways to strengthen your relationship with Him, find peace in His love and promises and fill your heart with even more faith in our Heavenly Father. Breathe in every word, breathe out every worry and savor each step you take with Him, always right by your side.

# *Where We are Needed Most*

Where we want to be in life and where God needs us to be are two different places. We may think we are ready to move forward, but God knows better and He keeps us exactly where we are. Or, when we think we have found our home, God asks us to pack our things and move even before we are settled in, knowing there is somewhere else we need to be. God can see every intricate detail of our lives and what lies ahead of us. When we see an opportunity, God may see danger and moves us in the opposite direction to avoid an absolute disaster. And when we feel we are headed down a road leading to failure, God is carefully and purposefully placing our steps along a winding and bumpy path, bringing us to our greatest of victories. We are always so anxious to know what the next step will be, where it will take us and want to get there without even taking it. But only God knows where our journey will take us next and when we are ready to get there. Wherever God has us in life is where we need to be and exactly where we are meant to be. Always wait on God's perfect timing, have faith in the plan He took His precious time writing and the storm we almost found ourselves in will turn into the blessing we can rest in.

## Always a Reason

There is nothing more contagious than a smile. When you receive one, without even thinking you give one back. They brighten the darkest of days and give others a chance to see a glimpse of the beauty of our Heavenly Father. Yet we deny all of the blessings our smile can bring by allowing the worries of this world to take it away. All of the reasons we have not to, will never outweigh the reasons we have to smile. Knowing the Creator of the Universe loves us, is protecting us and walking every step of our journey with us, should bring unspeakable joy and happiness to our heart. Not only do we have God's hands filling ours, we have His abundance of blessings overwhelming our lives. We just have to make the decision to look past the negativity we are constantly reminded of and right to the positive light God is shining all around us. Even on the days it is the hardest to smile, the blessings we have will always be greater than the burdens we carry making it impossible not to.

Philippians 4:13

# *Through Him We Can*

We often wonder what it would be like to have the strength of just one of God's arms to help us through our day. Just imagine the problems we would be able to solve if His thoughts replaced ours. The hurt we would be able to heal if we could stretch out His hand instead of ours would bring so much relief to so many. Imagining, wondering and longing to have enough strength, wisdom and love to accomplish all of these things is a waste of our time, because it is already ours.

Where our power ends, God overwhelms us with His, giving us more than we imagined we could ever have to overcome anything that comes our way. When confusion clouds and drains our thoughts, God overflows our minds with His and we receive the answers to questions we didn't even know we had. And when the faith we have in the healing power of the wounds of our Savior is greater than any hurt that is being felt, God's love will flow through our own hands and help all of those in need. We would never be able to contain God's strength, His thoughts or power. But when He is a part of our lives, minds and souls, He will supply us with just the amount we need at the very moment we need it. When we live our life for God and surrender ourselves to Him, we will be able to do all things through Him.

## *Through Our Eyes*

No one here on earth has ever seen God, or has a picture in their back pocket to show everyone. But we do not need a picture to know what God looks like. The love we pour out from our hearts paints a perfect portrait of God's. Our hands that are kept busy helping others display a precise image of the working hands of our Father. And as we use our words to encourage, uplift and offer a friendly smile to others, the precious reflection of God's Heavenly face that everyone longs to see is forever embedded in their minds. When we love endlessly, support and help others continuously and speak blessings over each other passionately, God is seen in each one of us. Open up and allow God to shine through your heart, your hard work and your smile. The picture that everyone so desperately wants to see will be revealed when they look at you.

# A Chance Worth Taking

The power of the decisions we make for our lives will never be left in our hands. That kind of power can only be held, contained and controlled by the hands of our Heavenly Father. Life can be heavy and the choices we are faced with can cause our hands to tremble and even break. And as the pieces fall apart, God catches each one and the choices that need to be made, that only His mind could make, bless us in ways ours never could. The game of life will ask us to take many chances, but there is only one that is necessary. Place your trust in God, have faith in His hands and the chance you thought you were taking, will be the choice you never end up regretting.

## Perfect Timing

Our life and the path we travel may not look like anything we had in mind. Our steps may lead us to the left, when all we want to do is go to the right. The destination we thought would be perfect for us to end up couldn't be further away from where we find ourselves and even further from the time we planned on being there. Through the ups and downs of life, we can always have faith that if we stay focused on God, follow His lead and allow Him to guide our steps, we will end up exactly where we need to be.

God's plan for our life is absolutely perfect. We may not see it right away or understand why He is taking us in certain directions, but we can boldly and courageously take every step knowing that God has gone before us, making our paths straight. Always make the choice to wait on God and His direction. His joy will be our strength and in His love, we will find our courage and direction. As we find peace by placing our faith in His perfect timing, God will find pleasure in rewarding us with His Heavenly treasures.

## *Free to Love*

The last thing we think about or even feel like doing when our heart is hurting and our hands are more than occupied fighting our own battle is to use our broken heart and busy hands to heal and help others. But this is exactly what God expects us to do. It's not that He thinks our hurt doesn't matter or our arms are strong enough to carry the burden of bigger battles than our own. When God nudges us to bring peace to a broken heart, He is telling us the hurt we so deeply feel has already been healed. And as He guides our steps directly onto the path of a battle that someone else is fighting, He is guaranteeing us that ours has already been won. Every hurt we feel and battle we face belongs to God. And as we let go, we free our hearts to share His love, our hands to provide His strength, and find that the greatest blessing we will receive is to be a blessing to someone else.

# Where Hope is Found

Even the smallest amount of hope is impossible to find some days. We have tried all we can and exhausted all of our efforts, but still do not see a way out of the prison of worry and stress we are being held captive in. Before we hang our head in defeat, we can raise it up in victory to our Father, where all of our hope comes from. He will always remind us of the promises He has made and intends to keep. His arms, that He wraps us up in, will provide the protection, strength and energy we need to overcome any obstacle that stands in our way.

His loving hands will reveal every piece of our brokenness that we have lost, and how carefully He is placing even the smallest of pieces back together. And as we place our faith in God, His love will overwhelm our lives and break us free from the chains the enemy thought would hold us down for good. When we have God, we will ALWAYS have hope. And when we have hope, we will always find rest, comfort and safety in the everlasting peace that could only come from above.

# Change is Good

Change isn't something we voluntarily sign up for. It never feels right, always brings uncertainty and at times unhappiness and makes us so uncomfortable that we even want to crawl out of the skin we were once content being in. But it is in these very moments when God is doing His greatest work within us. He is removing old thoughts from our minds to make room for new ways of using our gifts and talents to bless this world in ways our old ones never could.

His overpowering love is expanding our hearts so we can love more, give more and comfort more of His children who are in need. And the new path God is leading us on challenges us in ways we could never overcome on our own, giving our faith in Him an opportunity to grow and a chance to realize that a life without Him is impossible. We will never be able to experience all of the new blessings God has in store for us if we insist on holding on to our old ones and our old ways. Change will never be easy. But when we embrace it and accept the challenges that come along with it, the happiness that is brought to our lives and those around us will be more than worth it.

# When God is Your Guide

When we finally open our eyes to God's plan for our lives and allow our hearts to absorb each intricate detail when it is given, our excitement may cause us to jump ahead of Him. But God's plan does not come alone. It brings along very specific steps that need to be taken and a timeline purposefully and perfectly pieced together by the hands of our Father. When we start to take steps on our own and faster than God can place them before us, we will stumble more times than we care to and find ourselves falling more than we are walking.

Getting ahead of God will set us further back than where we started. But when we take His hand, follow Him one step at a time and enjoy and learn from each one, the blessings God is leading us to will always be better than the ones we thought we had to run to. Always surrender to God, His ways and His plans. He will always know better, the joy and happiness we experience will always be greater and God will be able to use us in ways our minds would never be able to imagine.

# *God is a Giver*

God is a giver. His mighty hands gave us life. His love provides us with the joy in our heart and peace in our souls. His endless treasures provide our every need and His mercy gives us a chance to start every day with a clean slate. He wants nothing more than to overwhelm our lives with the outpouring of His blessings. The best way we can honor our Father, be like our Father and love our Father is by doing exactly the same. The kind words we say give hope to an empty soul. The love we share brings a ray of light to the darkness of this world. Our treasures may not be many, but what we can give, will provide others with more than they ever had. And when you take the hurt that has been placed on your heart and use it to fuel and find words of forgiveness, you give yourself and others the gift of healing. Always give more than you take and God will always give more than you expected.

## *Which Way Do I Go?*

The millions of directions life has us traveling in will end up leading us nowhere. Right when we think we are headed in the right one and getting things accomplished, we find ourselves turned around, moved on to a different task and not exactly sure how we even got there. In the midst of all the chaos, a long deep breathe can make all the difference. Every one we take in should be filled with God's peace, love and calmness. And every breathe we let out should take our confusion, frustration and anger along with it. In that very moment, we will feel all of the worries fall from our minds and allow all of the good and positive thoughts and feelings to fall into their perfect place.

God doesn't want us wasting our time and energy running in circles trying to figure out which way to go. His plan is clear, easy to follow and given to us one step at a time. When we follow our map, we will get lost every time. But when God's hands are our compass, His voice is our guide and we are willing to follow His lead, we will always find our way to where He needs us to be.

# *What's Next??*

We spend a lot of time asking God "why?". We ask why do things have to happen like they do. We question why certain people have to leave our lives before we want them to or come into our lives when we least expect them, interrupting our normal routine that we are content with. Even if God took the time to answer each and every one of our million "why's?", we would never be able to comprehend His thoughts or understand His ways. God takes us through twists and turns, ups and downs and on paths that we would never think or care to travel on our own.

He knows where we need to be challenged, exactly where we need to fall and where He needs to be, to pick us back up. Every pain we feel along the way will come with a bigger purpose. Every burden we carry will bring a greater blessing and the people we are able to love or have to let go of, even when we think we don't want to, will change our lives in ways we would have never experienced if we made the decision of which road to take on our own. Instead of asking God "Why?" we should ask Him "What's Next?" and faithfully place our hand in His. His ways, His thoughts and His reasons my not make sense, but will always be better than the best of our own.

## A Beautiful Mind

Habits are easy to make, but never to break. The ways we find ourselves set in become our day to day routine. We never give much thought to, or put any effort into, changing them. But God didn't bless us with a beautiful mind at the slight chance we may use it when we decide our ways are becoming too boring to handle. Every challenge we face is an opportunity for us to step out of our comfort zone and use our minds like they have never been used before.

The people who are brought into our lives by the hands of our Father will stretch our thoughts, open doors to different ways of doing things and bring new life back to the old one we have been living. If we truly listen, accept and embrace each one, our habits will be forgotten, our ways will be lost and our lives, as we have known them, will never be the same. When we allow ourselves to think big and dream big, even bigger blessings will follow. Appreciate but let go of the old, welcome and take hold of the new. The beautiful mind we were always meant to discover and the abundant life God intended us to live, will never be wasted.

## Never Be Lonely

Being lonely does not always mean you are alone. You can be surrounded on all sides by those who love you the most, but somehow feel like there is not a soul around. You may see their lips moving and their teeth shining brightly as they smile. Yet the words they have spoken fall short of reaching your ears and your soul is longing to hear even the quietest sound of their laughter. And though there always seems to be a helping hand reaching out for you to hold, not one seems to fit yours in the way you need it to.

This type of loneliness is lonelier than most and will linger until you finally look to who is above not below. Only God can fill the emptiness that plagues your heart and relieve the worry that burdens your soul. The joy He brings to your life is everlasting and the hand He offers will always fit just right. Being surrounded by those who love you and want to help is a blessing, but they will never be able to provide all that God can on their own. If you feel alone in a world full of people, you forgot to invite the One who created it in. Once God and His love overwhelms your heart, you will see and feel those around you, hear and enjoy their laughter and always find the hand you were meant to hold.

## *Less Work, More Change*

We spend so much time and energy trying to help others as they are facing challenges or trying to heal their hurt. We work tirelessly day after day with no resolution. All we accomplish is using all we have, leaving us with nothing left for what they really need. Simply sitting next to someone while they work through the pain may be the comfort that lifts it from their broken heart. Placing your hand in theirs may give them the strength they need to keep going. And lending a listening ear without interruptions as they release their frustrations can bring the peace their soul has been yearning for. Time in your presence is the most valuable present you could possibly give someone. As the world is running around in circles, use all of your energy to be still. The less work you do, the more love you give. And the more love you give, the more lives you will change.

## The Spirit Speaks

Even though it may take only a few moments, not too much effort on our part and is our best defense against the enemy, there will be times when we find it impossible to pray. Our heart is heavy, our head is spinning with worry and the words that once came so easily are nowhere to be found. We feel hopeless and desperate and panic begins to set in. But all desperate times do not call for desperate measures. What they do a call for is something much simpler, complete submission to the Holy Spirit, who knows us better then we will ever know ourselves. Our prayers will be heard even before we find a way to say them.

The Holy Spirit will present each one in a way we never could. Before we can say Amen, Our Father will answer them in a way only He can. Prayers are not answered because of the words we say, but because we believe in the words that are said for us. Open your heart to the Holy Spirit, have faith in the prayers that are given and the words you weren't able to find, will always be heard.

# His Plan Prevails

It may seem like the odds are all stacked against us. Every way we turn, there is something going wrong, a new challenge to face, or a dead end we thought for sure would lead us to our destiny. But it really does not matter what is going on around us. All that matters is what is going on above us. There is nothing in this world that could stop the plan God has so carefully created for our lives. He will turn our every wrong into a right, our challenges into triumphs and the dead ends that hinder us into new beginnings that overwhelm us. The mighty hand of our Father will never grow weary or give up and will always take ours and guide us down the perfect path He has designed just for us. When we believe in God's plan and have faith in His hand, the odds will always end in our favor and His plan will always prevail.

# *Never Will We Falter*

Opening our hearts to God's love will allow them to love unconditionally. Anchoring our soul with His hope and our minds with God's thoughts will have us chasing our dreams passionately. When we rely on God's strength and fuel our bodies with His power, we will begin to live life fearlessly. God is always bigger than our biggest challenges and strong enough to hold us up when all we want to do is fall. We will never wake up to a day without Him or fall asleep without His army of Angels watching over us. As we fill every inch of ourselves with God's love, His thoughts and all of the strength He is more than willing to give, we will always be protected, loved and able to live a life full of joy and happiness. When the world gives us every reason to fall, God will ALWAYS be the reason we never will.

## *A Heart That Loves*

We are always quick to blame the heaviness we feel on the weight that comes along with the worries of this world. The anxiety from not having enough time, money or energy to meet the demands of our hectic lives will always be one of our reasons for being so drained and exhausted all of the time. While they do contribute to our hurt, it is not always what is laid on our body that weighs us down. It is the heaviness that is pressing on our heart that does. A heart overwhelmed by anger is one that can barely beat. A deep and calming breath will not be provided by one that is consumed by bitterness.

Carrying around these destructive emotions will never solve anything or make the situation better. They will only steal our joy from today and make it impossible to experience happiness in any of our tomorrows. Anger and bitterness will never hurt another heart as much as it hurts our own. But a heart that feels love and embraces joy will always be happy and willing to share. Once we let go of our hurt and welcome the healing it will bring, our hearts will give us a beat to dance to and a breath to rejoice in.

## *Steps of Faith*

Even on our best days, the enemy is lurking around every corner. He is waiting for the moment we completely let our guard down and his chance to steal every bit of joy we are immersed in. Never do we ever have to stop enjoying the blessings God has showered upon us or celebrating all of the wonderful things He has in store for us. We just need to remember to always be on watch and listening for the negative words, actions and thoughts the enemy always has to offer.

When our faith in our Father is greater than our fear of the unknown, we keep the enemy at bay. As we courageously continue down the path that has been laid before us, whether we are on the easy road or falling down a crooked path, we move even further away from his advances. And on the days when our strength is failing, we can rely on the arms of our Father to carry us through and lift us up out of any harm that was meant for us. The enemy can follow us around every turn. But when our eyes are open to his nonsense, our feet are moving confidently in faith and our courage and strength are fueled by God's love, he will never be able to keep up.

## *Only Good Thoughts*

Let's face it...being positive can be quite a tall challenge at times. As negativity rears its ugly head and the walls of worry start to close in, remaining joyful in our thoughts and words is not always at the top of our priority list. But it ALWAYS should be. Every small negative seed that is carefully planted as a thought in our minds becomes a much bigger word we speak over our lives. Before you know it, the seed that was once a thought that evolved into our words is now happening right before our eyes.

When we think negative, we speak negative and end up experiencing all of the negativity the enemy so desperately wants to destroy our lives with. Instead of watering his seeds with our worries, we need to remove them by planting our own of God's love, words and promises. And just like the negative ones, they will turn to the positive words we speak and will breathe life back into the lifeless situation we have been staring at for too long. Don't just hope for a good life, use your words to thank God for the good life you expect to live. He will always bless you with an even better one than you expected.

## Move Mountains

Jesus once told His disciples if their faith was even as small as a mustard seed, they would be able to move mountains. Really think about that. Just a little bit of faith can make an entire mountain move. So imagine what a whole lot of faith could do!!! We so desperately want our burdens to be turned to blessings and our messes to miracles, but insist on allowing our fear to overpower our faith and put limits on our limitless God. We have the Creator of the entire universe ready, willing and able to bless our lives in abundance. Until we are able to replace our fear with unwavering faith, we will never experience or enjoy the power and greatness of our Father in Heaven. The choice is ours. We can stare at the mountain in fear or tell it to move in faith, and God will always answer accordingly.

# A Whisper Away

We sometimes feel that God is so far away from us that He could never see what we are going through, hear our prayers or reach out a helping hand to pick us up when we have fallen. But the thoughts we have about Him being out of our reach are much farther away from the truth than He will ever be from us. God is so close to us that He knows the prayers we have hidden in the deepest place of our heart, even before we know them.

The words that are still thoughts being formed in our minds fall upon God's ears before they are even said. God does not watch over us from a million miles away. He is right by our sides, guiding our steps and is ready and willing to catch us way before we know we will fall. God will always answer before we call, hear our prayers before they are said and His arms will continuously provide us protection, support and guidance before we have the chance to ask.

## *Faith or Fear*

The fear that we experience and the faith we so desperately want to be filled with may seem like two completely different things. But they have more in common than we like to believe. Both require a lot of our time and energy, affect the decisions we make and how we live our lives. The one thing that separates us from living a life consumed by fear or faith is what we choose to fill our hearts, minds and souls with.

When we give all of our attention to the lies of the enemy and the worries of the world around us, we choose fear. But if we focus on God, His love and promises He will always keep, we decide to live a life of faith. And as we stand at the crossroads of faith and fear, we must remember faith moves mountains, while fear only builds them higher. Our faith will quiet all of our storms, while fear will make them louder. Faith in God unleashes His blessings, but fear will block every single one. Fear will put up a good fight, but will never stand a chance against our Heavenly Father. And when it stares us in the face and tells we can't, we can confidently stare right back and allow our faith to say "My God already has!"

# A Father's Love

As we walk through our journey of life, there will be times where we stumble, moments we fall and give in to temptations we fight so hard to resist. But no matter how many times we may fail at this thing called life, it never affects the way or how much we love all of those around us, especially our children. We do all we can to bring happiness to their lives, fulfill their needs and love them unconditionally with every piece of our hearts. If we, as imperfect beings, can love our families this much, just think about the love our perfect Father holds in His heart for us. And because of His Holiness, His overwhelming love and unending mercy, God will always fulfill each and every one of our needs over and above what we could ever imagine. As we take every opportunity to bless others with our love, giving all we have to give, Our Perfect Provider will always make sure we will always have more than enough to enjoy the life He intends for us to live.

# A Moment Makes a Lifetime

No matter how hard we try or how tight our grip is around them, the words we say can never be taken back. Whether they are said out of anger, frustration or hurt, the words that take us a moment to say, can cause a lifetime of pain for the one who took a moment to hear them. Our words should always lift others up and not bring them down. They should be the light that brightens the path of someone's dark journey and the love that fills a once vacant heart. Our words may seem harmless and go unnoticed, but are the most powerful weapons we should always use to help and not to hurt others. Choose your words out of love, kindness and encouragement. They will be the ones that only take a moment to say but bring a lifetime of happiness to the ones who are blessed hear them.

# Big or Small

From the very smallest to the biggest, every trial we face is a chance for our faith in our Father and our patience in His perfect timing to develop. We may not think losing our keys or getting lost without a map to follow are problems our mighty God wants to deal with. The truth is, He wants nothing more. God knows exactly where our keys are. He wants our trust to be in Him to reveal them to us instead of spending hours on top of hours trying to find them on our own. God knows exactly where we need to be at the exact moment we need to be there.

Our faith in Him should tell us, if we do lose our way, we are not lost. Rather, we have been redirected to a safer and more purposeful route by the loving and protective hands of our Father. The small trials will only lead us to greater tests of our faith and closer to God and His countless blessings. No care, concern, test or trial is too big or small for God. He can and expects to handle them all.

## From the Inside Out

With every passing day, it seems we have more places to go, people to see and things to do. The desire we have to make ends meet and keep up with this busy world will begin to take its toll, and our physical bodies will begin to crumble piece by exhausted piece. While we may be falling apart on the outside, God's mighty and loving hands are not only holding us together on the inside, but renewing the strength in our hearts, minds and souls with every new day we are blessed with.

Once we give up on relying on our strength alone, we will finally surrender to His powerful arms and allow them to carry us through our day. As we travel from one place to the next, we should always invite God to come with us, embrace and bless every person we meet with His kindness and never do anything without His help and guidance. With God's love in our hearts, words in our minds and hope filling our souls, our energy will be endless, our happiness contagious and the people we bless will be countless.

## Inspire with Love

During our journey, many people will come and go from our lives. Some will stay longer than others, and there will be those who leave a bigger impression on our hearts. Whether they stay for a day or forever, they were all placed on our paths at the exact moment they were meant to be there by the hands of our Heavenly Father. We never meet people by accident. Instead, we meet people who we need or who need us to help each other, love each other or even challenge each other to be the best we can possibly be.

Their stay may be as brief as a passing by, so we must take advantage of each moment and person by spreading God's love with a smile, kind word or action. Meetings are never by chance or coincidence, but full of purpose and meaning.

Embrace each person God blesses you with, giving all you can offer and receiving what they are willing to give in return. Most of all, find happiness in knowing the time you have given, God's love you have shared and the joy you spread may have inspired them to do the same.

# *Words of Advice*

It is easy for us to offer advice to those who are facing trials and challenges. But as we offer our words, we often follow them with "I know it is easier said than done". We may know what we would do, or want to do, and what we want others to do. But if we have never experienced their hurt or frustrations, our words are sometimes better left unsaid. Instead of using our words or what we have been through, we need to focus on our Savior, offer His words and allow His example to guide the path of others.

Jesus faced every temptation possible and experienced a kind of pain we could never imagine or care to. Through it all, He kept His mind, heart and soul focused on God, had faith in His divine plan and overcame every obstacle that stood in His way, even death. Because of this, we can take our problems, our temptations, failures and troubles to Him, confidently knowing that He will understand and open His forgiving heart to us. Jesus will provide us with everything we will need to pick ourselves and others back up, dust ourselves off and continue on our journeys, stronger and better than ever before. Whether we are seeking advice or giving it, we need to hold on to our words and seek the advice of our Savior. Allow Jesus to use His words, lead by His example and guide our steps to make all that may be wrong in our world right again.

# With All of Your Heart

God wants nothing more than for us to fill our lives and this world with love. It is His first Commandment, top priority and reason for giving us free will. We should pour out our love for Him for being our Good Father, for the blessings He has showered us with, and for the peace and joy it brings to our lives. With the endless supply He has given us, we should continue to spread our love to all of those around us through our thoughtful words and acts of kindness.

While we are quick to open our hearts and lend our hands to God and others, we are just as quick to close the door to our hearts and keep our hands too busy to love or help ourselves. We seem to skip right over the part where we are supposed to love our neighbors as we love ourselves. God sees how beautiful we are and how perfectly He has pieced each of us together. He assumes we have already fallen in love with His masterpiece. And until we turn God's assumption into our reality, we will never know how to truly love Him or anyone else. Loving ourselves and every part of who we are will calm our hearts, uplift our souls and bless this world in ways we never could before. Close your eyes to what you may see and open them up to the beauty God and this world is blessed with. Then, and only then, we will be able to love God passionately and others devotedly, all because we chose to love ourselves whole heartedly!

## *Always Worth It*

Loving someone is not always easy. But anything worth doing or fighting for, never is. That is why God filled our hearts with His love that will never fail, give up or run out on us. It protects our hearts from the negative feelings the enemy is always willing to offer. It brings hope to every hopeless situation and it gives us the strength to endure every challenge we are faced with. The love God has filled our hearts with doesn't come with expectations or limitations. It doesn't place blame or ask for anything in return. But it does make the darkness bright, the impossible possible and expects to be given at all times. When things are good, celebrate with your love. When times are tough, come to the battle with love leading the way. Always love when it is easy, and love even more when it hard because it is an absolute gift that is always worth fighting for.

## A Choice We Make

What if one day we woke up and made the choice to be happy? No matter what the day ahead had planned for us, our goal for that day was to be the happiest we could possibly be. Instead of complaining on the way to work, we would thank God for having a place to work. We'd focus on the positive, not the negative. Our words would be used to compliment others and not criticize, even when we do not feel our best. We would not allow our circumstances or the actions of others to steal our joy. We would make the choice to pour out even more love, to find peace in every situation we face and to show that a little bit of kindness really goes a long way.

By the end of the day, we would feel less tired, our shoulders would carry far less stress and frustration and we would realize we had more time to focus on God and all of the blessings He has surrounded us with. Life may always give us a reason to be upset or angry. But God will always make sure we have a reason to be happy. We should never allow the circumstances of life to determine our happiness. With God's love consuming our hearts, His arms surrounding our lives and His goodness following our days, we have no reason not to enjoy the life we have been given and be the happiest we can be with each day we are blessed to see.

## Love Takes Action

The words we write down on paper may bring peace and joy to those who read them, but may not be seen by all. The words we say may bring happiness to the ears they fall upon, but not everyone is listening. What will bless this world and leave the greatest, lasting impression on the hearts and lives of so many, are the things we do. Our actions are more powerful than any word that could ever be written or spoken. They bring our love to life and the kindness we share gives others the opportunity to experience the good-ness of our God. The words we have written can be erased and the ones we have said can be forgotten. But our actions of love can never be undone. Choose to be a "doer", not just a "sayer" of God's precious word because actions will always speak louder than your words.

# *Refuse to Give*

We all have people in our lives who seem to take more than we offer. We give a little of our time, and they ask for more. We provide our help, here and there, and end up becoming a full time volunteer. We try to limit what we give and end up giving up all we have. The devil is no different. We start by giving him the smallest place in our minds for his worries and lies. Day by day, that tiny space grows bigger and bigger and before we know it we are completely consumed with his negative thoughts, words and feelings.

The only way to avoid his master plan to take over our lives is to stop it before it starts. The enemy spends every minute of every day looking for his chance to steal our happiness and joy. We must spend every minute of our day refusing his advances. If we never place our offer on the table, the enemy will never have the chance to take more than we are willing to give.

## The Light of Love

They may not be our finest or proudest moments, but it is safe to say we all have had times where we may have not wanted things to go well for others. Whether we were jealous, fearful of them moving forward without us or just having an off day, we didn't put our all into encouraging others to give their all. We must remember, life is not about competition, having more than or being better than others.

Life is about allowing God's love and light to shine so brightly through us so we can be the very best we can be, and help others do the same. Hearts that pour out love receive even more love in return. Words and actions that provoke kindness and generosity are always heard and open the door to an outpouring of God's love and goodness. And when our hands are reaching out to help, they will always overflow with more than enough to share with all of those around us. Blessing this world with Our Father's love, following His ways and only speaking His encouraging and inspiring words will take our, not so good moments, and always turn them into our best.

# Where We Need to Be

Our minds are always seventeen steps ahead of our bodies. Half of the time we are not even sure where we are or what we are doing because we are thinking about where we have to be in three days and what we will be doing in four. We begin to run this crazy race of to-dos and jumping ahead of where we need to be. Before long, we find ourselves tripped up and on the ground, not even knowing how we got there. When life gets to be too much, stress is burdening our hearts and worry is weighing heavy on our minds, we need to walk away from it all.

Not to give up and give in, but to spend some time where God can ease our minds and reassure our hearts that He has everything under control. When we are with God, we are never alone and always taken care of. We only chose to be alone and in harm's way when we get ahead of Him,

His plans and leave time for ourselves out of our day. Even when we think we don't have it or just don't want to take it, time alone with God, filling our hearts with His love and our minds with His words is what we will always need. He will make sure our minds match our steps, our plans follow His and we are exactly where our hearts and minds need to be.

## Mean What You Say

So many things get left unsaid because we allow our anger to speak over our kindness. Our frustration begins to scream at the top of our lungs, words we do not mean and reduce the loving words our heart wants to say to a whisper. We are so quick to speak that we do not take the time to really listen to what others have to say. We get upset over things we think we heard, but were never actually said. Before words are spoken, think about how they will sound. Allow yourself to feel what will be felt when those words are received. Give yourself time to really listen, not to what others are saying with their lips, but what they so desperately want to say with their hearts. Always listen first, answer with words filled with God's love second, and never allow anger to get in the way of hearing what is actually said, and saying what is actually meant.

## Always on His Mind

Every now and again, a name of an old friend or a family member we have not seen in a while is placed on our hearts. We begin to think about them, maybe even reach out to them and plan a day to see them. We know we should take the time to talk to them more often, but our schedules and to do lists always seem to get in the way. With all of the people in this world and the to do list He has, it must be the same for God, right? We think we may cross His mind every once in a while and He only gets around to listening to and answering our prayers when His schedule permits.

But this couldn't be further from the truth. Every moment of every day, we are on God's mind. Our names are forever on His lips and His ears are always open to our prayers. The love He has for us overwhelms His heart and His mighty hands will continuously provide us His strength, power and protection. The number of thoughts God has for us is far greater than we could ever count and each one is filled with the kind of pride only a Father could posses. Never an afterthought, but always His first, we are forever on God's mind, in His heart and taken care of, just as He has always promised.

# Temptations with Purpose

Every day we will be faced with temptation from the enemy. As soon as we find the strength to close one door, another one opens within seconds with something new to entice the needs and wants of our flesh. Although He allows us to be faced with these challenges, temptation is never something that comes from God. He lets us face our earthly desires to strengthen our faith in, and reliance on, Him.

It will be His mighty hands that help us close one door and His power that will carry us to and through the next. Even though we may feel like we will never be able to stand against the enemy's advances, God will never allow us to face or go through something that is much too difficult for us to handle. He will direct our paths to it, give us the confidence and courage to stand

against it and always give us everything we will
ever need to see our way through it.

# Who are You Chasing?

There are many things in life that will take us to the point of complete exhaustion. Tackling an impossible to do list, taking on more than we can handle and pretending to be OK when we are the farthest from it, are just a few. But what will take our breath away, stop our feet from moving and leave us broken beyond repair is chasing after anything or anyone other than God. We may think we know what and who will make us whole and waste so much of the precious time we have been given trying to catch up with them.

But God knows us better than we will ever know ourselves and keeps them just out of our reach for a reason. He knows the to do list we need to focus on, exactly what our hands can handle and where every broken piece has fallen and how to put them back together. When God comes first,

His Angels will follow and help us along the way. Our eyes will begin to see His plan come together right before them and we will have everything we will ever need to fulfill our purpose and bless so many along the way. When we chase after God, our feet will never fail, every breath we take in will breathe out His praise and who we truly need and what will make us complete will stand before us, close enough to reach.

# With Weakness Comes Strength

Life has become such a competition these days. We try to keep up with this fast paced world only to fall apart the moment we think no one is looking. We find so much shame in our weakness and failures that we would rather exhaust all of our efforts and energy on pretending to have it all together than ask for help. But we have it all wrong. It is in our weak, broken and vulnerable moments where we find all of the strength we will ever need in our Heavenly Father. God created us to rely on Him, lean on Him and need Him every day of our lives. He never wanted us to do any part of this life on our own. He wants nothing more than for us to take His hand and allow His love and power to carry us through each day we are given. God's strength is more than we will ever need. All we have to do is allow ourselves to need it. As we accept and embrace our weakness, we will find the more broken we are, the more perfect God's strength will be.

## Never Lose Hope

If we truly know who our God is, what He has done, continues to do for us and how much He loves us, why are we not overflowing with hope and faith that no matter what we face, He will always see us through? If we truly understand with every trial we face, a testimony will unfold and every burden we carry is a blessing in disguise, why do we allow worry and stress to overtake our lives? And if we absolutely believe, without a shadow of a doubt, that prayer is the most powerful and meaningful conversation we could ever have, why do we insist on wasting our time complaining about our problems instead of praying about them?

It is simple. The enemy is in a constant battle to take over our hearts and minds. Unfortunately, he is successful at times, leaving us hopeless, trying to fix our problems on our own and we forget we have the ability and privilege to communicate with the one who will win the battle each and every time. With whatever circumstances we face, refuse to give up hope, wait on God's timing and always keep praying. Our hope will bring us peace, our patience will lead us to God's blessings and our prayers will always be answered.

## Heals Every Hurt

The pain the disciples felt as they watched Jesus suffer and die on the cross had to be unbearable. The sorrow they experienced as their teacher, best friend and mentor was taken away from them was probably something they expected to feel for the rest of their lives. But just as Jesus had promised to them over and over again, the pain they felt and the burdens of sorrow they carried would all be left behind them, along with every tear that had been shed. Through the gift of the Holy Spirit and the comfort they received, they were able to pick themselves back up and enjoy every day they were given by spreading God's love and promises to all of those around them.

Throughout our lives, we too will experience loss, sorrow and pain. But through the promises of our Father and the faith we have in His love, we know before long our sorrow will again be turned into joy. When tears are falling faster than rain drops during a storm, remember with every rain that falls, there is always a rainbow waiting for us to enjoy on the other side.

## *The Control is Ours*

Negative thoughts and feelings will weigh us down more than any other burden we will carry throughout our lives. They will consume us, drain all of our energy and steal precious moments of our day we can never get back. These feelings and thoughts just don't appear out of thin air. They are purposefully placed within our hearts and minds at the hands of the enemy with the intention of causing us hurt and pain. He wants nothing more than to be responsible for ruining our lives and will stop at nothing to make sure he is victorious. But he can only get so far with a master plan that is compiled of lies. Once we realize he is the source of these feelings, we can allow ourselves to feel them, but let them go before they become a part of us. And when we do, the heaviness and hurt they caused will begin to subside. Once we make the decision to be in control of our feelings, our negative feelings and the lies they were built on will never be able to control us.

## *Already Done*

How many miracles do you think we miss out on because we simply do not believe they are happening? Far too many for us to count! We will spend endless hours and days asking God for His Divine intervention, for His hands to do only what they can possibly do. But the moment He takes our impossible and makes it possible, we do not believe what is happening right before our eyes. God does spend endless hours and days listening to our prayers. And even before we have finished presenting them, He has a plan in place to fulfill each one that will be revealed in His perfect timing and according to His will. This world and its troubles are far too great for us to handle, but never stand a chance against our Heavenly Father. Have faith in God, trust in who He is and what He can do and know, when the Creator of the Universe says He will, it has already been done.

# A Text to God

Our prayers are like text messages we send to God. No matter how far or close we are to Him, we can be certain that every one we send, will be received. Of course, they will have typos, and even some missing words. But as the Holy Spirit as His autocorrect, God will understand each and every one. As quick as we are to send them, we want the exact response we expected sent back even quicker. But the control of how and when our messages are answered is not ours, and the same thing goes for our prayers.

With a perfect plan in place, God will always have an answer to give to every prayer He hears when the timing is just right. It may not be the response we wanted or expected and far from the time we wanted it. But it will always be exactly what we need at the exact moment we need it. Even when our fingers grow tired and words are hard to find, we should continually and faithfully send our "messages" to God. He will always receive them and will be able to read every word, even the missing ones. With a response that will exceed your highest of expectations, God will always answer when He knows you are ready to hear what He has to say.

## *More than Expected*

When we look through the clouds that are darkening our day and focus on our Father, we will always see His Heavenly light shine through each one. His steady hand will not only bring calm after the storm, but will overwhelm us with His peace during even the most destructive ones. And when our faith in God is stronger than our fear to take a step we do not see, we will find our greatest of blessings will come from our most difficult challenges. Whether we are given the whole picture, or the smallest piece of it, God's plan for our lives is perfect. As we follow His lead with praise on our lips and faith in our heart, seeing it will no longer matter as we begin to experience it. Not always easy, but always worth it, we should always take each step that God places before us. When we trust in God's hand, He will reveal His plan that will always be better than expected.

## Challenges Bring Change

Trading in our plans for God's can be a scary thing. Ours may keep us exactly where we want to be and surrounded by the people we feel we would never be able to live without. God's may take us away from the job we love or place we live, far from the people we think we need and change us in ways that will make it impossible to remain who we are. As the fear of the unknown begins to settle in, we can continue to walk our journey with confidence and faith in the One who not only knows the way, but has pieced it together with His careful and loving hands. God knows each and every precious gift He has placed so deeply within our hearts, exactly where they are needed the most and will bring us there when it is time.

The people who walk our journey with us and those who veer off of our path are being guided by our Father. His mighty hand will always bring us who we need and remove those we may not, when the moment is right. The challenges that overwhelm us will be the ones that forever change us, allow us to fulfill our purpose here on earth and have always been a part of God's plan. We can run towards them instead of away from them knowing God is with us as we take each step, making sure they will always end in our favor. The life we want to live and the life God has intended for us to live will never be the same. But when we open our hearts to His, take His hand in faith and follow wherever He may lead, we will find, God's is always better.

## Expect Answers

When we find ourselves facing a difficult situation, the part we find easiest is presenting our case and needs to God. We know the challenges we face, how we would like our story to end and we ask God to help us. What we find most difficult is trying to avoid speaking negative words over our situation or the people involved. If our hearts are doubting while our lips are praying, we are blocking God from answering the very prayers we just got done saying. We must believe with our entire existence that God is more than willing and able of not just answering our prayers, but going above and beyond what we could have possibly imagined. Then and only then will we see and experience the over-whelming power of our almighty God.

## *Say and Receive*

The negative voices we allow to run rampant in our head overpower the positive ones that are screaming at the top of their lungs in desperation, never giving them a chance to be heard. Our only hope of silencing these destructive noises is hearing, receiving and embracing the uplifting and loving words of others. Just hearing someone's "you can" can make our "you can't" disappear, giving us every reason to try again.

The encouraging words that are spoken from a friend's heart can erase the discouraging ones the enemy has placed so deeply on ours. And when we take the words that have been spoken to us and bless the lives of others, we give their hurt a chance to heal, their soul a chance to be filled with hope, and their heart a chance to feel the kind of love that could only come from above. When God gives you a loving word to speak, always say it, and when that word is given back, receive it. He knows exactly what needs to be said and what needs to be heard at the exact moment it is needed most.

.

# Avoid Damage

There are so many different things that will fight for the attention of one of the most precious gifts God has given us. Day in and day out, the negative feelings of the enemy, the material temptations that surround us and the love others seem a little too willing to give, pull and tug at our heart, looking to take full ownership. No matter which one comes out victorious, they will all leave it with some type of damage. The enemy will deflate our heart of all of its hope. The things of this world will be taken away, leaving it empty. And the love that was so eagerly given is just as eagerly taken back and will leave our heart broken in pieces.

If we first fill ourselves with God's love, His word and promises before anything else can stake its claim, we will avoid the damage even before it has the chance to start. What we allow in our hearts is what we will give to others, what we receive in return, and will have the final say in us living a blessed or burdened life. The key to our heart rests in our hands and it is up to us who we unlock it for. Guard it, protect it and choose to give it the love only a Good Father like ours can give.

## He Holds the Pieces

Even before we began our lives here on earth, God had a very specific plan and purpose for us. With each day we are given and every step we take, another piece of the puzzle of God's master plan is put into its perfect place. There will be days where we feel like the pieces have fallen apart and moments where we feel like the pieces we do have, will never fit together. Sometimes the puzzle is missing a piece and we give up on it ever being complete. We need to find peace in knowing that it was never our job to look for and find the pieces or put them together. God already knows where each one is and where they go and would never allow our pieces to fall apart without a way to put them back together even better than the way they were before. We should always trust and believe in the plan that God has placed in our heart and follow His lead no matter where it may take us. Regardless of how broken our puzzle may look, God and His faithfulness will always complete it in the end.

## Our Part is Faith

Throughout our lives, we will face many battles. Whether they are emotional, physical or mental, they all have one thing in common. They were never ours to begin with. Each battle we face, God has led us there with a purpose. Some will place our faith under just the right amount of pressure to help it gain the strength it needs for us to succeed. Others will provide us with the right words to write our testimony that will bless the lives of others as they stand in their battlefield. And every trial we face shapes us a little more into the person God has so perfectly planned for us to be. God knows who He is, what He can do and the blessings He has in store for us on the other side of this challenge. As we stand against an army of many, we can have faith in our army of One who will lead us through every battle His mighty hands have already conquered.

## Love is Patient

God's love for us is absolutely perfect. It is so great, so pure and surrounds us throughout all the days of our lives. But there is one aspect of His love that will help us hold on to our joy and let go of our worry. It is patience. God knows we are not perfect, that we will stumble and fall at times, and even when we try so desperately to take control of our lives, He patiently loves us anyway. God's love keeps Him so patient that He can wait without worry for us to call on Him for help, lean on Him for strength and give up our ways to follow His. If God can be ever so patient with us, we can allow His love to overtake our lives and have the same patience with those we love in ours. And when we overwhelm our hearts with His love, we can have faith that His timing is always perfect and patiently wait for Him to place each step of our journey before us. Once we understand, accept and share God's love, we can live patiently, peacefully and expectantly as we wait for His perfect plan for our lives to unfold.

# Blessings Come By Faith

Jesus has told us over and over again that if we just believe, we would see all of the glory of our Heavenly Father. Instead, we decide to put our worry before worship, and allow the negative thoughts of the enemy to overpower and overtake the love and peace God has so graciously given us. We have a God who is ready and willing to shower us with His blessings, be with us and guide each and every step we take on our journeys. Yet we fall short of receiving and seeing it all because we refuse to believe. If we focus on who our faith is in and not on the fear that is presented before us, we will never have to worry or be afraid for the rest of our lives. When the road ahead of us is too hard to see and we are not sure where it will lead, choose to step out in faith. God's hand will always be waiting to lead us to the blessings He has been ready and so willing to give.

## *To Give is to Receive*

When we spend our days worrying about having our own needs met and keeping things for ourselves instead sharing with others, we are telling God we have no confidence in His ability to provide for us. We are allowing our fear of not having enough to be greater than the faith we have in our Heavenly Provider. Putting our trust and security in things we store up on earth instead of in God will always leave us empty handed. But if we take what we have in our hands now and bless others by fulfilling their needs, we will always have more than we could have ever asked for. God wants us to enjoy our lives and share His love and joy with the world through our generosity. When we open our hearts, give our time, love and treasures to those around us, we just make more room for God to shower us with more of His blessings. God has more than enough to give; we just have to make enough room to receive!

# Gifts to Share

Life would be absolutely perfect if we were just good at everything, right? Time would never be wasted, there would never be any obstacles to overcome and we would never have to ask any one for help or advice. This perfect life we think we were living would end up being the miserable one we would soon be regretting. Each of us has been blessed with specific gifts that will help fulfill the purpose God has so carefully planned for us.

The ones we find ourselves without will be discovered within someone else. The very moment we need that person, God places them directly on our path to bless our lives in a way only they possibly can. The time you spend with them, the challenges you face together and the perfect advice they are so willing to give will never be experienced if we could handle it all on our own. Our gifts would lose their purpose, our life would lose its meaning and our hearts that find so much happiness in blessing others would be lost of all of their feeling. We should always appreciate and share all of the gifts God has showered us with and THANK Him for everything He hasn't. The precious moments we have with the special people He gives will bring perfection to the life we live.

# Last Words

As Jesus departed from this earth, and visited His disciples for the final time, He left them with His most precious final words. With all of the passion and love that consumed His heart, He told them to go out to all of the nations and spread His word, all He has taught them and share His goodness and mercy, blessing their lives in abundance. Not only was He talking to His disciples, He was speaking these words and placing them deep within each one of us. Every new day we are given is a new opportunity to bring the light of Christ to the lives of others. The smile we give, the kind word we say and the compassion we show and share with those around us may be just what they need to know that Jesus is with them or remind them He will never ever leave them. We may be the one and only way others will ever know the greatness of our God, forever changing their lives. With Jesus right by our sides, we can be His voice, share His love and be the bright light this dark world so desperately needs.

# About the Author

With a stop watch in one hand and a pen in the other, Tara has dedicated her life to helping others change theirs. After renting a brief space in the teaching field, a short stay in the world of broadcasting and a much too long journey down the sales road, Tara found her home in the place where most people only visit a few times a year, the gym.

Her passion for helping others has kept her there for five years. The lives she has touched and changed and the lifelong friends she has gained will keep her there for many more.

But her true calling was brought back to life when she traded her broken plans in for the perfect plans of Our Father above and is the reason this book exists today. From a very young age, Tara has written stories and poems that brought happiness to the eyes of whoever read them. Those stories turned to passion filled wedding vows, heartfelt speeches and after facing one endless battle after another, she surrendered her life to God and began to write devotionals overflowing with faith and love for Him that turned her battles in to blessings for her life and so many others.

After years of just getting by in life on her own, Tara is now enjoying life and blessing the lives of others even more by living a flourishing life with and for God. He has blessed her with a loving and supportive family, including two children who are the center of her world. Surrounded by their love and with God guiding her steps, Tara is embracing the journey she has found herself on.

With her passion for God fueling her soul and His endless love overwhelming her heart, she has written each and every word on these pages to bring you closer to God and bless you with the peace He has showered her life with.

Her 1st book:

You can reach Tara for conversation, sharing to order books or for speaking engagements via:

Email: followwhereheleads@yahoo.com
Facebook: https://www.facebook.com/TaraAltheide
Twitter: @altheide_tara